Degrees of Twilight

Maggie Butt

Published by The London Magazine
11 Queen's Gate
London
SW7 5EL
United Kingdom

Copyright c 2015 Maggie Butt

The right of Maggie Butt to be identified
as the author of this work has been asserted by her in accordance with
the Copyright, Designs and Patents Act 1988.

ISBN 978-0-9926061-5-2

Printed in Great Britain by Imprint Digital, Devon

Design and typesetting by Shane Ellis

All rights reserved. This book contains material protected
under International and Federal Copyright Laws and Treaties.
Any unauthorised reprint or use of this material is prohibited.
No part of this book may be reproduced or transmitted in any form
or by any means, electronic or mechanical, including photocopying,
recording, or by any information storage and retrieval system without
express written permission from the author / publisher.

Find out more about The London Magazine at:
Thelondonmagazine.org/tlm-editions

Contents

The Archaeology of Hotel Rooms	1
Time Travellers	2
Degrees of Twilight	4
Travelling Backwards	6
Clock Shop	7
Behind Me	8
Oakfield Road	9
Survival	10
The New Mothers	11
Comfrey	12
Mapping Bow Bells	13
Walls	14
Mum and Dad, 1934	16
This is How the Generations Pull Apart	17
Memories	17
It All Goes On	18
Go Gentle	19
The end	20
Lying In	22
Death Valley	24
The Next Winter	24
What Remains	25
Letting Go	26
Airborne	27
Ellis Island, New York.	28
Top Of The Empire State	30
Bad Fingerprints	31

An Englishwoman of a Certain Age	32
Today I Didn't See the Giant Buddha	33
Cuba 2008	34
The Other Holy Places of Umbria	37
Etruscan cemetery, Orvieto	40
Naming	41
Whitstable 2010	42
Hringvegur Snow	44
After the Holiday	45
The Working Day Commences	46
The Pros and Cons	47
Variance Analysis	48
Risk Assessment	49
Do Not Pass Go	50
The Photographer Predicts	51
Pain	52
Unfinished	56
Burning Bush	57
The Why of Shells	58
Meltwater	59
In Praise of Beaches	60
Replete	61
In Sunlight	61
Cherries	62
Blue Moon	63
Wish	64

Acknowledgements:

Thanks to the editors for first publication
of some of these poems or versions of them:

Accounting, Auditing and Accountability Journal;
Acumen Literary Journal; Artemis; Axon: Creative Explorations; Envoi;
Equinox; Ink, Sweat and Tears; London Grip; Magma; Meniscus;
Message in a Bottle; Orbis; Poetry News; Quattrocento; Snakeskin;
Text; The Bow Wow Shop; The French Literary Review;
The London Magazine; The Shop.

'Meltwater' in *Feeling the Pressure Poetry
and Science of Climate Change*
ed Paul Munden, (British Council)
2008 and *Read to Succeed* (Longman USA) 2009

'Airborne' and 'Mum and Dad 1934'
in *Poetic Pilgrimages* University of Salzburg 2011

'Go Gentle' and 'This is How the Generations Pull Apart'
in *The Book of Love and Loss* (The Belgrave Press) 2014

'Hringegur Snow' in *Outlook Variable* (Grey Hen) 2014

'Lake Trasimeno' in *The Editor* (Rockingham Press)

'Walls' was placed in the Torbay Poetry Competition
and 'Pain' in the Second Light long poem competition

Thanks for inspiration to Philip Gross for
'The Why of Shells'; to Hylda Sims for 'Cherries';
to Graham Mort for 'Pain'

Thanks to June Hall and to the Palmers Green Stanza group
for close reading, enthusiasm and great advice

**Previous Publications
by Maggie Butt:**

Poetry:

Quintana Roo, Acumen Publishing,
2003

Lipstick, Greenwich Exchange,
2007

I am the Sphinx (e-book and mp3) Snakeskin,
2009

petite, Hearing Eye,
2010

Ally Pally Prison Camp, Oversteps Books,
2011

Sancti-Clandestini–Undercover Saints,
Ward-Wood Publishing
2012

Non-Fiction:
Story: The Heart of the Matter, Greenwich Exchange,
2007

> "But at my back I always hear
> Time's wingèd chariot hurrying near"
>
> Andrew Marvell
> To His Coy Mistress

For Joan and Alfred Brookes, overtaken by time,
but with gratitude and love, as ever;

and for Tim, Amy and Katie,
who make every moment precious.

The Archaeology of Hotel Rooms

It's almost always August in hotels,
and always present tense. Owned and occupied,
without past or future; our breath fills its space.
Layers fine as millefeuille, sweet with sugar dust,
pot-shards and fragments, photo-bright.

The surface is Moroccan silk, harem-scarlet
shot with sunset gold, the hum of air-conditioning,
comforting as money. Storks clack like football rattles
on the roof – sign of good luck, as if I didn't
smell the deep spice of it – saffron, turmeric, paprika.

Peel back years like faded floral wallpaper,
good fortune pasted on good fortune.
Find a wide room for families, small dormitory
of watchfulness, blue with Italian light
detail of sleeping faces, fine as an old master.

Down to a Paris room where flowerprint grew over
walls and ceiling, door-back, curtains, counterpane.
A room with no way out, where none was wanted;
this space held everything there was, hot-house
of universe and time, love's here and now.

Sift softly, blow those grains, flick squirrel brush,
back to the first, foreign with the unknown smell
of garlic, which loitered like a stranger on the stairs.
Baroque figures winked down on me in bolstered bed
cloaks flying, into the unknown summers.

Time Travellers

The sick are well, dead smiling, old are young,
framed photos bloom on windowsills and walls,
I am a baby, arms aloft to be picked up
time zig-zags like a running man avoiding bullets.

Framed photos bloom on windowsills and walls
I am veiled bride, gowned graduate, new mum,
time zig-zags like a running man avoiding bullets
listen to the echoes of our laughter.

I am veiled bride, gowned graduate, new mum,
we are in Venice with our grown-up daughters
listen to the echoes of our laughter
I am a girl, in cotton frock with poodle-print,

We are in Venice with our grown-up daughters,
three straw-haired nieces squint into the sun,
I am a girl, in cotton frock with poodle-print.
Faces unwrinkle, hair turns luxuriant and brown

three straw-haired nieces squint into the sun,
a bunch of snowdrops, roses, autumn leaves.
Faces unwrinkle, hair turns luxuriant and brown
he's in a de-mob suit, leaving the war behind,

a bunch of snowdrops, roses, autumn leaves.
Mum is a red-cross nurse, dad like a movie star
he's in a de-mob suit, leaving the war behind
futures latent as a roll of undeveloped film.

Mum is a red-cross nurse, dad like a movie star
I am a baby, arms aloft to be picked up
futures latent as a roll of undeveloped film,
the sick are well, dead smiling, old are young.

Degrees of Twilight

Twilight is defined according to the sun's angle below the horizon: 6º below - civil twilight, 12º below - nautical twilight, 18 º below - astronomical twilight

6º Civil Twilight

The shrill of the park-keeper's whistle
summons night, creeping like a panther
stalking deer, without a twig cracking:
pad, pad, only its eyes glinting.
Abandoning our game, we streak for the gates
watched now from every bush and shadow.
Panting, we plan ahead: if the gates are shut
will we attempt to climb (oh, the slip of bars,
the spikes on top, the dizzy fall) or try to find
that fox-hole in the fence which used to be
behind the big oak tree? Any way to flee
the gnarled hobgoblins of the dark,
escape into tungsten and fire.

12º Nautical Twilight

On land, white flowers would vibrate
with urgency in the borders, insist their white
upon the eye. Trees and houses would blacken
to silhouette against an ultraviolet sky.
Out here, a blueing of the light across the sea
and sky, curved with the curvature of earth.
These moments with both horizon and stars in view,
before a gradual losing, cobalt to navy.
Light ebbs away like energy,
like memory, till more is gone than left.

18º Astronomical Twilight

One by one, the stars reveal themselves
in slow strip-tease, as if they were not always there
underneath the brilliance. Glimmers of small
compensations, way finders, hints of a populated
vastness, a depth of understanding hidden
by the glare of day, reminders of our smallness,
of the length of time it takes their spark to reach us,
dimming across distances, of the shortness
of twilight, the closeness of night.

Travelling Backwards

Low sun rakes the fields, highlights
furrows of earth opened to frost;
hedges neatly trimmed, crouched
low in preparation for winter;
trees, losing leaves, readying
themselves to become sculptures.

I've always booked forward-facing,
eager for the outskirts of new towns,
for lakes flung with clouds, for marching
windmills, a white horse guarding a hill.

But now, hurtling towards winter
and twilight, with the passing
farms hereandgone hereandgone
I might reserve backward facing -
watch the open country of the past
spread itself far as the eye can see.

Clock Shop

Half-timbered shop with flagstone floors
where time is valued, weighed and priced: a yard
of minutes, pound of hours, seconds by the quart.

The clock-shop keeper holds the keys,
repairs the rifts in time, its unpredictability.
A wind-up world where nearly-there is good enough.

Never in silence, never alone, crowded
with the tushing -shushing of their sleepless whispering;
unsyncopated hearts, each tapping out its homely beat.

As we step inside, a welcome cry, the fastest
skips ahead to chime the hour, high and merry,
unrestrained, and at their leisure, in their own time

one by one the others follow suit, echoing deep
or long the simple one, two, three of afternoon,
a one, two, three of flannel-suited bright young things

filling hours with tennis, a one, two, three
of housemaids hurrying to boil up pots of tea,
a one, two, three of bank-the-fire for early winter dark.

The chorus of clear voices fades away
and falls to whispering again, taking their cue from
grandfathers with their smooth gold faces, on guard

around the walls, beating tortoise slow, waiting
for something to start or end, unhurried,
as if every second wasn't measured, sounded, told.

Behind Me

Here I am again, fumbling
to dress in the dark and cold,
reluctant as a dormouse from its nest,
off to work before the roads
are clogged with cars. Weary.

But today, I glimpse them
from the corner of my eye,
my grandmothers and all
my great-grandmothers,
up before dawn, shawls
pulled around their shoulders,
off to mills and factories
and scrubbing other peoples
floors. Their strength
reinforces my bones.

We fill the kettle, glance
at the last star, fierce
in an indigo sky; we fuel
ourselves with jam and tea;
we brush our hair, arrange
our public face and pull
the front door closed, quietly,
not to wake the family.

We step into another day
where the sky lightens.

Oakfield Road

I faithfully repeated it, then learned to spell
i before e, the road I'd be returned to
if ever I was lost, where everything
would be all right and in its place:
each tile on the black-and-white
star-checkered path; the velvet density
of moss in clinker-built garden walls;
grape hyacinths edging the lawn with blue;
at six-o-clock the click of the gate latch
dad home from work, tea on the table,
i always before e.

Survival

(For Daisy)

Once, death was a familiar figure,
in his shirt-sleeves at the kitchen
table, or lying companionably in the bed
between a man and wife, hampering
the work of midwives at each birth,
bending over cradles in chill dawns.

He hovers round you now, cranes
his neck beyond the nurse who guards
and nourishes all day and night, longs
to unplug monitors, twist drips, stem
oxygen, licks his lips at your fragility,
waits to claim you as his own.

But the legion armed with microscopes
and stethoscopes are at your side.
They gift you strength to send him
slouching off into the dawn, and you sit up,
comb your elfin hair, smile a young girl's
hopeful smile, resplendent in survival.

The New Mothers

We sat and cried that third day, concrete-breasted
torn and stitched. We cried for love which opens
and closes like a fist, flooding caves within the heart.

(Our tears a free-fall leap of waterfall from jungle cliff,
the fury of a summer storm, dashing down petals,
a bone-cold drenching in rivulets along the scalp.)

We cried relief to find ourselves and you alive, breathing
past the pain. We cried for those before, mothers
in mossy churchyards, or coffins shoe-box small.

(Our tears the steady pour of winter down a drain-pipe,
the leak of roof to overflowing buckets, bowls and dishes,
the ceaseless night-long drip of worn-out-washer tap.)

We cried for all the falls we can't womb you against:
the bully teachers, failures, phone calls in the night
beyond our arms. We paid up-front in tears.

Comfrey

My mother's mothers planted Knit-bone
in the yards of mill-towns' back-to-backs,
watered country wisdom, passed it on
to girls uprooted between worlds.

The mashed-up pulp of Comfrey root
smeared as a paste around a broken limb
will harden to a cast, supporting bones
to mend them straight and true.

Tiny bell-flowers flecked with soot,
hairy leaves large as a man's hand,
(his strength to break or hug) a wedding
heirloom to each daughter-bride -

a hunk of Bruise-wort root for each new wife,
newspaper wrapped Black-wort, a turnip
with a coal-caked crust, pale fleshy inside,
out of its element, oozing sticky tears,

transplants her to a woman's world
where Comfrey's bitter tea might cure
when remedies were few, if love would risk it all;
might poison others, speed them to the earth.

The leaf too looks two ways: the rough
will draw the putrefaction from a wound,
while smooth side soothes and heals:
most potent if it's picked while just in bud.

Mapping Bow Bells

The great bell swings skywards, upturns,
before its weight tips it, falling towards
the clamour of its cry. And down below
standing on blocks, the ringers wait, pull, count
the delay, let go as rope flies up the tower,
catch it on the drop. Down on the holy ground
it names the hours and days, finds out the faithful.

My grandmother was born within its sound
blessed with its livery, imprinted with its voice,
rooted in this city of pealing bells, when steeples
spiked the skies. Its tolling was the background
of her childhood in the terraced clay-brick streets,
- its familiar song so close it went unnoticed
as a steady heart-beat, always carried with her.

And now my daughter maps the pattern of its call
how outside street din swallows up its toll
muffles a peal which once reached to the hills
- now few can hear its deep refrain ("I do not know,"
says the great bell of Bow); enfolded, like my voice
which called her in from play, lit the candle to light
her to bed, offered her oranges and lemons.

Walls

Once there was only me, princess and peach.
Then there was him, who needed a name
and my subjects called on me to choose it.

He lay in a carrycot beside me in the car;
ugly and red, and mine. Soon
I tried to put a pillow over his face.

Later we played parachutes or pirates;
bruises and blood, but I ran my fastest
when he lay injured in the infants' playground.

* * *

In one weekend of DIY, the board partition
rose across our room, bisected the bay window,
introduced 'privacy.' My side was papered

with girls in pink meringue petticoats,
twirling parasols. His side was blue with steel
and speed: cars and boats and jets.

At night, we couldn't settle in our silken cells,
unused to solitary confinement,
so now we talked. They came in continually

scolding us quiet. I whispered stories
to send him to sleep. Talk was our new touch,
our new sight, breaching the night wall.

* * *

My life swung open on a hinge of luck.
The girls with parasols drove off
in soft top cars, climbed aboard yachts,
discovered they had wings and flew.

His roads were blocked by fallen rocks;
jet engines coughed; his boats becalmed
or beached. I talk and talk but can no longer
make out his reply, walled in silence.

Walls can be nibbled away by wind and rain;
smashed by a giant iron ball,
torn down in jubilant revolution,
toppled by trumpeters.

Mum and Dad, 1934

(After Sharon Olds.)

I see you at the wrought iron gates
of your schools, tipped out, half-grown,
towards the gates of piece-work factories,
earning-a-living, the-rest-of-your-lives.

Learning clangs shut behind you
and I want to shout, "Don't worry
you can choose your own books now,
stand in the gods at theatres, spend

every lunch hour in the British Museum,
take coach trips to exotic cities."
I want to tell you your grandchildren
will go to University, have everything.

But I would also have to tell you
the price of this new world
and all those who will not return
from the darkness in-between.

This is How the Generations Pull Apart

My daughter's hand is dragged from mine
by the weight and press of commuters
on the Moscow underground - heedless,
uncaring of her smallness and my panic
as the doors close between us.

Now mum drifts in and out of sleep,
in and out of herself, her hand slipping
from mine in slow motion. No knowing
if there's a station further down the line
where she might watch for me.

Memories

Trains pass in tunnels
brightly lit faces; glimpses
which rattle away.

It All Goes On

As grey dawn trickles round the sick-room blind
couples on cliff tops watch the sun go down,
a spear of crocus breaks the icy ground,
party-girls whoop and whirl to *Dancing Queen*.

Couples on cliff tops watch the sun go down
while you sip icy water through a straw.
Party-girls whoop and whirl to *Dancing Queen*,
an infant class will learn to forward roll.

While you sip icy water through a straw
kids perch on harbour walls with fish and chips,
an infant class will learn to forward roll.
While you're befuddled-blind on drip fed drugs

kids perch on harbour walls with fish and chips,
half-faint from dieting, brides breathe "I do."
While you're befuddled-blind on drip-fed drugs
he proudly paints the sign on his new shop.

Half-faint from dieting, brides breathe "I do,"
a spear of crocus breaks the icy ground,
he proudly paints the sign on his new shop
as grey dawn trickles round the sick-room blind.

Go Gentle

(In argument with Dylan Thomas.)

Why not go gentle into that good night
like drifting into sleep from sun-soaked day,
remembering the brightness of the light?

Weary of gross indignities, take flight,
wave off the drugs, dementia, slow decay,
why not go gentle into that good night?

Good housewives, who have polished fiercely bright
both floors and faces, earned this holiday
remembering the brightness of the light.

Wild women who could drink and dance all night
flop down and kick your achy shoes away,
why not go gentle into that good night?

Grave women, who face death with failing sight
let memory fling you back from this cold clay
remembering the brightness of the light.

And you my mother, there on the sad height,
dive cleanly from your tower of fear, I pray.
Why not go gentle into that good night,
remembering the brightness of the light?

The end

begins with a call, like call to prayer,
a clamour of bells, wake-up alarm.
Alarm! Alarm! At the end of the phone
The nurse says carefully, "Come now."
And my pulse drums *Coming! Coming!*

The front door bangs, running heels clack,
tube doors swish open and close,
open and close, like the chambers
of your weary heart. Girls chat
about tomorrow, as if it will come.

Out in the air, and racing, feet pound
the pavement's chest, my breath hoarse
as a cough, blood crashes in waves
against traffic's rumble and wheeze.
A woman with a suitcase holds out her hand

to halt me, ask the way, the time,
as if I knew. But I can't stop, calling
to her over my shoulder, "I'm sorry.
Sorry." Pigeons startle and take off,
the murmuration of their wings

lifts like a prayer. At your bedside
machines still whirr and beep faint
reassurance, so perhaps you hear
my voice, my tumbled promises, my love?
Your voice the first I heard,
and mine your last, circling like that flight
of pigeons, calling down the years.

(After Sharon Olds.)

Lying In

Who knew how long the crossing takes?
The ferryman paid, but rowing so slowly
you can trail your fingers in the water
see the little fishes rise to nibble them,
circles upon circles radiating from their O mouths.

***

Which labour is the hardest work, the deepest pain?
The one which pushed your children into light
or this, which delivers you to the dark?

Both marked by breathing, harsh and fierce,
and effort which contorts your face;
both leading to an unknown world.

In pregnancy you ate for two
bequeathed your liquorice addiction;
soon I must live for two.

Then, you lay three days in a side ward, alone
in labour's agony and fear. So I won't leave you now
however many hours and days this takes.

Afterwards it will be my turn to carry you
furled safe inside me
for as long as my heart beats.

***

Night sounds: the tick of the wall clock,
counting something meaningless, tick, tick, tick;

the rasp, pant, wheeze of your breathing,
the long gaps where you practice stopping;

far away outside, a blackbird's song defies
the dark, anticipates one final dawn.

Death Valley

Slumped in the saddle now and entering
the badlands; dust kicked up by horses hooves,
dust in the eyes, dust on the tongue.

A high sun bleaches oxygen from the air,
hazes each rock into shapes of regret;
each cactus spiny with recrimination.

No hiding place here from myself,
and desolation ready to let loose a volley
of arrows anytime from the ridge.

Misery's swarm of flies circle my head;
however fast I move, batting them,
they travel with me, a buzzing cloud.

Nothing to do but tip my hat against
the sun and flies. Lick cracked lips.
Plod on. Plod on. Plod through.

The Next Winter

The hat you knitted,
Christmas gift of velvet scarf.
Love's warmth in steel winds.

What Remains

I have stood by the graves of dead kings
carved in marble, their feet resting
on lions or dogs, according to the violence

of their end; gothic tracery around their crowns,
palaces in miniature, mottos and heraldic
beasts. Lying quiet now beside them,

queens who had been uprooted and sold
across the world, for profit or for peace,
who may or may not have cried at his demise.

I have entered sepulchres, pyramids,
catacombs, dolmens and cairns; read
gravestones, which speak of love and hope.

I have wandered in Moorish palaces
echoing with piano music, mists
enveloping the carvings, dripping

from the sword-tips of palm leaves;
purple damask and velvet rotted,
books in the library eaten by tropic damp.

I have read inscriptions by wealthy men
about themselves, carved in their lifetime,
listing their glories and mourning families.

I have considered the things which remain:
coins, smoke-blackened oil lamps, a table leg.
A sandal, a belt buckle, a thimble. A verse.

Letting Go

Although I wobbled when Dad's steady hand
released the saddle's back, I freewheeled
on downhill into the rush of flying's thrill.
And teaching me to swim, he held me
by the puppet-strings formed by my costume's
criss-cross straps; and though I felt him leaving go
I kicked away, trusting my body and the water's lift.

But now that it's my turn, my grip is glued,
stiff fingers must be prised back one by one.
I failed to learn the trick of letting go
of stale regrets, false pride, maternal frets,
my looks, ambitions, or my dearest dead.
I'm tethered fast, a sand-bagged air balloon.
Oh, teach me to rise weightless in the blue!

Airborne

Every now and then
when you had quite forgotten
you were sitting in an iron boat
sailing incongruously through the blue
dispersing clouds like ice-bergs -

Every now and then
when you had quite forgotten
how the very fact of it defies
the laws of nature, stretches
imagination thin as pizza dough -

Every now and then
when you thought life
was drifting along pretty nicely
kids and job and all
the seat belt light chimes on -

Every now and then
the whole thing gives a lurch
shakes like jelly beans in a can
drops your stomach 27 floors
in freefall elevator -

Just to remind you.

Every now and then.

Ellis Island, New York.

We grip the frozen handrail of the ferry,
watch the waters churn their silver song.

The seagulls teach their young to ride
the wind, hover at head-height, hoping

for scraps, catching them in flight, tasting
anticipation in this welcome-harbour's air.

Now just us tourists, seeing once-removed
through camera's lens, knowing how memory

can trick and lie. But every immigrant is here
behind our eyes, dressed in their desperation

and their optimism; watching the raised arm
of liberty (modelled on the sculptor's mother –

who better to open the door to this new home?)
They search the crowds for ghosts they left behind:

see how she flicks her hair, the set of his
shoulders, tap of her fingers, curve of his head.

The boat hull bumps and tears the wooden piers
of Ellis Island, they clutch the rails, fling

their old life to the tide, climb gang-plank
to a land which seems to roll and heave,

lift ashore their bundled clothes and words
the recipes and songs, tucking them close

as gold coins sewn into the hems of petticoats
wrapped with memories like old woollen shawls.

Top Of The Empire State

Manhattan's lights spread out below -
this firework show of wealth and power
outburns the feeble stars. But watch
them flickering from this high tower

and know that each breathes its own life:
last girl to leave her office sighs
and cuts the lights; while vest-clad man
in gloomy kitchen rubs his eyes

opens his empty fridge and blinks;
drunk clubbers, frantic megawatt,
flash out their neon mating signs;
soft night-lights shimmer round a cot;

old couple doze within the blue
of TV screen – can't stay awake;
flushed, sticky-fingered six-year-old
blows out the candles on her cake.

A glowing web of living lights,
though most have never brightly shone,
un-valued till you mark their loss
dark windows where the flame has gone.

Bad Fingerprints

I was held by Homeland Security -
the only blonde-haired, pearl-wearing,
unveiled woman, the only person
with confidence in the by-ways
of the English language, its freeways
and unlit no-through-roads.

The officer with the scraped-back hair
and a bulging holster at each hip
eyeballed me: "You've got bad fingerprints,"
my fingertips dry as the mouths
of the speechless Hijabi women,
"Should have moisturized on the plane."

Not their fingerprint reader at fault
but me who was bad: like a bottle of gone-off
milk, like Michael Jackson, like a badge,
a curse, a thrill. What should I do with
my new-found badness? Rob banks
and fool forensics with impenetrable prints?

Best to start small – ignore the Big Issue seller,
fail to give up my seat, swim out beyond
the coastguard's flags, give tourists false
directions, cheat at the self-checkout - badness
spreading from my fingertips up my arms,
pumping in my veins, blackening my heart.

**An Englishwoman of a Certain Age Visits New York
for the First Time and is Thrilled to be Invited to a Greenwich
Village Poetry Reading**

I imagine it will be like the 60's:
Dylan, collar up, face framed with curls
might shamble in, guitar across his back
slump in a smoke-filled corner, and we
would all be cool, pretend we didn't see.

        ***

Smoking is banned, but there are sofas
in a curtained section, half-clandestine
as a glimpse of underwear. Breathing
tastes of coffee, rippling the senses
sitting them up to beg like perky dogs.

The poet rises, gravely takes the mike,
"This poem is in 'Urban Molecule' magazine."
the audience yap appreciation, barking
affirmation - a kennel of Jack Russells:
"In this poem the words are backwards." *Ruff!*

Stifling our mirth, we escape when we can -
runaways to the crisp night air, the yellow
cabs, the poem of streets, their weave
of rich-familiar names: Lexington, Bleeker,
Broadway, Bowery, Fifth. *Woof, woof*

Today I Didn't See the Giant Buddha

The time was late, the tide was wrong, the date was inauspicious and so I missed the choppy ferry ride between container ships lying offshore like floating towns behind jutting green islands; I missed an English lighthouse on a sugar-loaf rock in the South China Sea, small boats steaming every which way leaving the purposeful dashes of their foamy wakes, clouds tall as sky-scrapers, the spittle flecks of breaking waves; I missed the long climb up 298 steps in air so humid I could drink it, drenching hair and running rivulets down the small of my back, air hot enough to warm me at next winter's bus stop; I missed the stalls selling bright silk purses, shirts, pyjamas, table runners, golden waving cats, jade dragons, laughing Buddhas, joss sticks, sunglasses; I missed the shaved-head monks and nuns in saffron and mustard, the tiny prayer bells catching a thin breeze lifting from the sea; I missed raising my eyes, squinting against the sun, to the massive bronze feet and thighs, the folds of coppery cloth, and far above, his face and curling hair; missed wondering how heavy how fired how poured how raised how smoothed how venerated; missed turning back down the steps into the noisy world, knowing I had seen the tallest seated Buddha on the planet.

Cuba 2008

1)
It isn't just the tail-finned Cadillacs and Chevys,
Che's face on every wall - not just the uninvented
shelves of micro-chipped consumer goods -
not just the queues and shortages, make-do-
and-mend, where even in a grand hotel
the taps run dry; here children play in car-free roads
with marbles, cardboard boxes, footballs,
home-made skateboards, mirroring the games
I played. Cuba is my childhood with the heat
turned up, the beat turned up, a longed for land
of sunshine every day, still living out a dream
that people can be equal. Sees how it winds
the clockwork of my rusty revolutionary heart.

2)
We have our bad days and our good - me and the cars –
the morning sun which shows our paintwork dented
and re-touched, owing much to filler; our hours of wheezing
up the hills, our crunching gears and clanking undercarriage;
but on our best days, when the light is kind, photograph
our style: our sleek tail-fins and fine upholstery; feel our power,
the thrum of engines built to go the long haul.

3)
In our hotel, Capone reserved whole floors,
away from prohibition and the reach of law;
cigar smoke spiralled to high ceilings,
gangsters opened windows, hoping for cool breezes
from the sea; Mulatto girls were willing, for a buck,
and rum like treacle fuelled the sticky nights.

4)
Grey is banished from this technicolour world
where cars are painted raspberry, kingfisher,
gold; where oil pumps nod like patient parrots,
feathered scarlet and green; and lofty palms
spike from the canopy of trees. Tall girls with skin
of caramel and molasses have high-stepped
from a chorus line to strut the Tropicana stage
in high-heeled ruby slippers, spangled costumes.
A director, who is never satisfied, re-lights
the Caribbean every hour, palest aqua, wash
of turquoise, midnight blue; closes the credits
with Cuba's wealth: topaz, sapphire, lapis,
handfuls of flung diamonds.

5)
This cask was brewed and what ran out
was music; spilling from houses, cars,
a band at every corner café: here Spain
ferments with Africa, flamenco mates with tribal
drums, slave-voices raised in suffering
counterpoint the clack of castanets;
Pied Pipers with bongo, guro, tres-guitar
trance me in rhythm: salsa, rumba,
samba, reggae, and Cuba sashays
like an adolescent girl, takes her first
sip, tipsy with promise, sways hips
to the beat of what's to come.

6)
On this broad, tree-lined street, five couples tango
to a tempo slow as turning of the years, pressed
close and winding round each other, gliding
on the marble pavement, deep in the music
and each other's heat, unaware of washing hanging
from the paint-peeled balconies, of pot-holed
pavements, four generations in one flat, lit by
bare bulbs, windows with bars instead of glass,
lost in the revolutions of the dance.

The Other Holy Places of Umbria

Fonti del Clittunno

Willows bow down and poplars raise
their arms around clear pools, astonishing
blue at deepest depths, as if Kingfishers
have dived and given up their turquoise
essence at a spring which bubbles
for the river goddess, old as faith.

Perugia Cathedral

Among the suited, sunglassed men, heavy
with threatening aftershave, one younger,
knowingly handsome, with long wavy hair,
pauses to check his own reflection
in the smoked glass doors to the Duomo.

British and Commonwealth War Graves Cemetery, Rivotorno

Assisi is strung like a rosary of pink and cream
around the hill where Francis prayed for peace
and preached to ancestors of birds who sing
here now in this green field below the town
where neat rows of white marble stones
etch silent names and messages, *a corner
of a foreign field... and at the going down
of the sun... he was our world... and love
from mother.* And bones of boys sigh into the soil.

Portonovo

White pebbles chosen from snow-dazzle beach
where time is measured in the rhythm of small waves
sucking back the shingle. They speak of long-slow
humbling in waves to conjure smoothness; how small
the precious thing may be, picked from a beach of millions.

One stone, palmful of heaviness, curved smooth
by tides. One circular and flat, the third an egg,
laid by an mythic reptile, laden with promise.
The fourth is chipped, and there within, a gallery of stars,
a diving depth of quartz, worlds within worlds.

Montefalco I

Magnolia: a tree of pale cupped female hands
raised in supplication, waiting for the rain.

Each petal as it falls resembles a silk slipper
the pattern for a Roman oil lamp, ready for light.

Montefalco II

The fire-flies flash and flicker
round us in the jasmine scented
dark. A holiness of nightingales
within an olive grove.

Lake Trasimeno

open the window
let the dawn-rinsed air rush in
with a river of song

along the lake shore
light amplified by water
peace unfolds its wings

Etruscan cemetery, Orvieto

Neat rows of tombs, unsealed and long defiled
gape wide as slack jawed skulls, while tides of green
have lapped into their rocky coves, a wash
of moss and fern and ivy in their humid hearts.

Town of the dead, with swept, paved streets;
a downward flight of steps behind each door.
Town of the loved, of houses built to last
a thousand years, to withstand earthquake,

war and the slow mounding up of earth.
Town of gods long since eclipsed, snuffed out.
Town of echoes and a hush of leaves,
a whir of wings, a bird's lament, the twitch

of lizard in dry grass, the ghosts who ask,
*What did you do with my love? I laid her here
with oil and spice. I built a home and carved
her name over the door.* A town of eyes

at my back, whispering and whispering,
*Where has my love gone? Where
has she gone?* Overhead the careless
blue, and underfoot the stone-heart earth.

Naming

Words lose their currency, strung
like a hammock between two languages,
swaying in the stippled shade
of a Puglian *olivio*, which has soaked up
more sunshine and weathered
more winters than I have.

I name the butterflies which sip
from the *lavanda*, painting the air
with movement and light, spiralling in pairs:
winking eye, tiger's breath, fired sunlight.
Their proper names are fixed in Latin,
words netted and pinned to a felt board.

In the cool of early *mattina*, a retired engineer
with a soft broom dusts spider's webs
from the *lavanda*, so, as the sun rises higher,
the butterflies can dip and twirl in safety.
And she who named me, no longer
there at home to tell it to. *Cara mia.*

Language stutters and defeats me.
I listen instead to the secrets of wind
in the leaves; a Warbler's underwater flute
like a bird-whistle on sale in a *mercato*;
the teasing lure of the Golden Oriele
"Find me now, seek me now, name me now."

Whitstable 2010

I'm down the beach among the Kentish
geezers with their shaved-head kids
who hurl rocks into shallow waves
and at their brother's heads.

Mums hunker by the seaweed-festooned
groyne with beer and plastic bags
of sandwiches, spurn suncream,
tattooed backs and meaty cleavages

broiled red-raw, ignore the screams
of tough small girls in polkadot
pink swimsuits, nan teaching them
to fish for crabs off the breakwater.

I doze, secure as if I fitted in their world
as oysters in their shells, safe with *The Family
from One End Street*, parlance unposhed
by time, echoes off terraced houses where

my dad grew up, accents sharp as lathes,
dropped t's and h's littering the shore.
A whelk-weaned family, aspiration-free,
can stick two fingers at the rest,

sit back to watch the dinghies tack
against the wind, seagulls hang
suspended in the sky, the sea creep
forward up the shingle - as it was,

is now and ever shall be. Half in a dream
I hear them laying bets: if the incoming
tide will wake me first, or the shower
from their traditional wet dog.

Hringvegur Snow

First it falls featherly   silence and stealth
layering crunchiness   capturing light
counterpanes countryside   smudges the sky
restful on weary eyes   prayerfully white.

Turns to a tempest   hurls itself howling
wild at the windscreen   blinding the bend
erases the road ahead   car at the cliff-edge
whirls up the white-out   which waits at the end.

After the Holiday

Work comes thundering in again
like a great wave across a flat of sand.

I'm lost as cocklers in Morecambe Bay,
King John's crown jewels in The Wash,

when the tide breaks over me,
its army of hooves and spears

spinning me this way and that
caught up, another piece of flotsam,

tossed junk, buffeted by the jetsam
of other shipwrecks, loose timbers,

planks and masts and packing cases,
crashing and churning in the surf

and I am submerging and rising
gasping again for air.

The Working Day Commences

I wake early in the paddock with the sleeping
lions. A muscle twitches under a tawny flank.
A tufted tail flicks at a fly. The sun rises.
I turn to creep back into dreams but a heavy head
lifts and yawns, and then another, shaking
a sleepy mane. And one by one they struggle
to their feet, their amber eyes fixed on me,
and at my back a silent fence rises between me
and the open country of sleep. The lions advance
with their deliberate paws and ready teeth.

The Pros and Cons

Work wakes me from sleep, flicking
the soles of my feet, squeezing cold water
from a sponge into the neck of my pyjamas.

Early, in the cold before the central heating,
I change course for work, steaming like a ship
breasting the ice-bergs, cutting through.

Work eats my life, chewing slowly
in the dark - a minotaur, savouring
my hours like new arrivals of virgins.

And yet I welcome work – let it distract
my losses and my fears, soak them up
like bread clearing the plate of gravy.

Variance Analysis

For Tim, i.m. Fred

The hours go slow and yawn and scratch themselves
and we are naming parts of balance sheets,
tight in a windowless room, totting the cost,
while the first day of spring unfurls outside;
and you are motorbiking scented country lanes
absorbing this year's deficit – its countless loss.

Fluorescent tubes hum songs of swarming bees,
no breath of blossom in this air-recycled room
no sun with surplus warmth, awakening assets
no daffodils turning heads to drink the light.
While you are chopping logs: axe-gleam, sweat,
pine-smell, chips flying, piling contingency.

I'm reckoning the fast depreciation of my day.
Doves coo on chimneys, primed for production,
cat stretches in a patch of golden afternoon,
ponds thrash till frogspawn bubbles up its yearly yield;
and you are in the garden, planting onion sets
thumbing each into the damp soil, balancing life.

Risk Assessment

Dress up your superstitions with new names,
the future is a cliff edge in the dark.
Seem scientific, plan insurance claims,
dress up your superstitions with new names,
cast runes, deal tarot, hear the stars' refrain.
However much you plan, the truth is stark,
dress up your superstitions with new names,
the future is a cliff edge in the dark.

Do Not Pass Go

A red dot on Free Parking was the clue
that worlds-away in Leeds a girl at Waddington's
had boxed a huge Get Out of Gaol Free card,
the chance to step back into Baker Street.
The Red Cross parcel's tins of margarine
and processed cheese were grabbed
to feed their grinding hunger, but Monopoly
was opened gingerly - to feed their fragile hope.

A sentry posted on the hut, the game afoot.
Mayfair-level banknotes for every country
they'd creep through, folded in the pile of top-hat
money. A compass. Silk maps stuffed in the hotels,
imprinted with the railway routes which chug
across a continent towards the sooty scent
and rush hour roar of Fenchurch Street; the hills
and rivers which split the Stalag from the Strand;
dark forests and wide plains which open
to the Old Kent Road. Do Not Pass Go.

The Photographer Predicts

Vilnius, 1936

Spruced up in best clothes, your family returns
my camera's steady gaze, looking into a future
of familiar hopes and household fears; the worst
an angry neighbour, sickly child, or jilted bride.

Instead the Russians will deported you all
to an icy labour camp, and you will smuggle
a spoonful of Lithuanian soil in a drawstring bag
in your underwear and carry it always.

You will scratch letters home on birch-bark,
copy out miniature prayers on paper
cut from cement bags and bind them into a book,
embroider a handkerchief, using a fish-bone.

Elena Kirlyte will roll bread morsels between
her finger-tips, form delicate beads reminiscent
of amber. She will dry them, pierce and thread
and knot them into a forbidden rosary.

You will carve a cross to wear around your neck
from the handle of a white plastic toothbrush,
so the strong young adults might return home.
Look this way please now, and smile.

*In the 1940's about 300,000 Lithuanians were
deported to Soviet Labour camps.*

Pain

I wait like a scorpion in a hole, alert
inside you, from forehead to funny-bone,

nose to knee, on the tip of your tongue,
deep in the rotting roots of your teeth;

sleeping snug within your body's cave
so you barely know I'm there, rarely

a twitch, a snore, until you stumble on me
in the dark and I turn, teeth bare,

eyes fire, a mountain troll, wolf,
bear, dragon - claws glint, ready to rip

you from your senses; I turn on you
quicker than snake bite, tiger-pounce,

faster than spark and tick, a thing of
zip and zing, of flash and flare,

fizzing like a firework, shooting
star, straight to the grunt and groan,

a morse code signal, sunlight sparked
off mirror, forked lightening fingering

church steeple; unguaged, uncaged,
my calibrations set well beyond necessity

or sense, far into cruelty, dark and malicious,
licking my dry lips; one jab would be enough

to make you drop the hot pan, pull back
the bread knife, straighten your back,

but I don't ever want to stop; I'll skid
towards the precipice with no brakes,

crash through the town like a runaway bus;
from stab to twisty knife, heat up like molten rock

a lava flow, volcano erupting, erupting, erupting;
best mates with death, rabble rousing

carousing, we stumble through the streets
of some unwary medieval town

on wild stag weekends, I'm herald
and gatekeeper to his ultimate good night;

I gather like the first leaves turning over
as the hurricane approaches, I spin and lift you,

twist and knot like a rubber band, shoot fire
through your nerves until you don't know

whether to stand or lie or sit or scream;
and you can't share me, even love can't feel

the molten metal of another's agony,
blazing and untouchable, white fire;

and yet my memory is slippery,
an absence, an amputated limb, reminder

of the ghost of me but empty as a polo mint,
an imprint, a snow angel, a disused church

hollow and echoing with itself; and I'm
invisible beneath a microscope, in a Hedron

Collider, in paint, in clay, on photographic
plates, not a glimmer, a whimper, a trace,

not a butterfly's wing of me, dandelion seed
of me, grain of salt of me, nothing, nada, nix;

I slip along the waterways of A-delta and C-Fibre
like water snake, darting fish, silver and gone,

your canals and rivers open to me, undammable,
the Severn Bore wave, tearing upstream;

I'm the slavemaster you can't escape
or buy your freedom from, standing

over you with whip tapping at my
well-shined boot, watch you sweat, revel

in your powerlessness, for you are chained
to me, owned by me, body and blood;

I'm fiddler, flautist, pied piper, running
my fingers up and down scales,

making you hop like an Irish dancer,
jerk into a jig, do the twist, head-spin

and break-dance to my screechy discords,
boogie to bruise and blister and bee-sting,

cry to the magnificent major chord of C;
and when the door swings wide on 101

I'm the only one in sight, the bottom line,
the end of the road, the black toad

crouching in the dark, the last lover
who stands and opens his arms to you.

Unfinished

Six hundred years since Michelanglo
started to chip away a slave, straining
for freedom, muscles bulging on torso
and arm, head twisted, tugging for liberty.
Then, called to Rome, abandoned him
half woken, stuck as a fly in amber,
fighting to release himself from marble.

In the next gallery, a muted fresco,
Christ in his rough-hewn tomb, struggling
to sit up, head and shoulders slumped
in pain, weighed down with the world's
suffering, wounds and bruises throbbing,
half-alive and longing for that untroubled,
numbing sleep he has surrendered.

The slave interred in marble doesn't hear
his warning tears of grief and separation.
He chooses life, each drop of agony and joy:
to yawn his yet unfinished yawn, stretch like a cat,
flex his rigid muscles, feel his skin against
another's, rain pour down his face, to run
until his heart bangs in his chest, lungs burn; feel it all.

Accademia Gallery, Firenze.
"The Awakening Slave" Michelangelo Buonarroti;
"Christ As The Man of Sorrows" Andrea del Sarto.

Burning Bush

A curious choice
for the all-powerful Lord of Hosts
to speak through
a burning bush;
when he could have gone for
rolling thunder, say,
or the blanketing silence of snowfall.

Maybe it was a grudge he had been harbouring
since Creation
against a peculiarly ugly shrub,
designed just before tea-time on the sixth day
when his concentration wavered.
The Bible is not specific on horticultural particulars.

The flames lick up, hot on the face,
and the bush is not consumed.

Perhaps he liked to hear his voice
made gravelly by smoke
like a jazz singer?

Or was he trying to warn Moses
that men who say
they've heard the voice of God
are playing with fire?

The Why of Shells

The where and when are lost in currents, cries
of sea-gulls, drying salt on sun-warmed rocks,
minute extrusion on a coral reef or sandbank,
unfathomed in the sweep of lighthouse beam.

The what is chinked in every childhood's bucket
bent-for in the foaming waves around the toes
picked-out among the high-tide sea-weed debris
coned and swirled or clammed shut in protective pairs.

The how inborn within a cell-brained greyish slug
which carves the ridges, ripples, pastel shades,
without precision tools or jeweller's eyeglass,
or pigment crushed from rarest beetles/sepals/gems.

The why starts well: with armour plating, shields,
the practicalities - falters and wavers before the why
of shape, the why of beauty. Whisper the question
to its cold and creamy curves. Put it to your ear and hush.

Meltwater

My time is coming, smell it on the wind
watch raindrops winnowing down glass

touch ice-cube to your lips and tongue
feel the cool chemistry of meltwater

see me submerge fields and swallow crops
spill out of wells to infiltrate your graves

raising the dead; firm ground will swamp
to ooze and squelch and slip, mud-symphony

hear gurgles, trickles, runnels in your sleep
reach for the drifting flotsam of your dreams

sweep river-sludge and sewage from the rug
swell my boundaries with your salt tears;

heave seas, wide breaths to rear up hills
waves come to claim their lost inheritance

listen to the future: rain-rocked, lake-like
nothing divides the waters from the waters.

In Praise of Beaches

For they fill and empty with human tide
For wives of fishermen have watched upon them
For hollyhocks and valerian may flower upon them
For they have the power to make me lie down and rest
For the incoming tide will not let me oversleep
For they give leave for us to read in public
For the air is thick with the salted words
For they smell of coconut and ice cream
For they add crunch to sandwiches
For the generations may mix freely
For girls shall anoint each other's backs with oil
For children may shriek without reprimand
For students check into them in lieu of hotel rooms
For sun umbrellas shall blossom in primary-school colours
For the shade of an umbrella is enough
For they have necessitated the invention of the wind-break
For bodies of all shapes are unabashed
For one may compare one's thighs, both favourably and unfavourably
For they come in flavours of pebble, shingle and sand
For they may be black, white, yellow or red
For they glitter with the powder of seashells
For small clouds shall pretend to be smoke-signals
For sunsets stain them implausible shades of fuchsia and gold
For light-houses may wink protectively over them
For they lend themselves to walking and thinking
For plovers will pity the curlews' lament
For the unwanted and forgotten is washed up on them
For the terminally lonely may leave their clothes in a neat pile

Replete

Enough of beauty - I have devoured
small boats curtseying at anchor,
green palace-dotted hills swarming
the spice-scented shore of Asia Minor.

I couldn't chew another mouthful
of waves, scything and winnowing light
with the wash of every passing craft,
and each heave of the ocean's breath.

Well, maybe just one last taste,
seasoned with a pinch of myrrh:
the taxi driver says, 'Today hot
but slow, slow, winter comes..."

In Sunlight

The shadow
of the hawk
is black
on the water.

Cherries

A quarter pound of cherries
and a book, beside the sea,
the shuck of waves on pebbles
the racing clouds, and me

the sea as glazed and languid
as a mile of satin sheets
the pips lined up along the groyne
small seeds of future sweets

a cherry for each poem
bursting on the tongue
a tide of calm is at the flood
a harvest of songs sung

and some of them are bright as blood
and some as warm as wine
but each is sweet as summer's flight
and all of them are mine.

Blue Moon

31.12.2009

Sometimes the day you long for turns as sour
as month-old Yak's milk, while the one you dread
blows in with floral breath. And this New Year
as party plans cocked-up, I sulked, remembered
past Lang Synes, not tuneful but heart-felt,
champagne and fireworks. Flat as sunk soufflé
I grumped "I'd rather go to bed at ten
than watch a fakey TV hogmanay."

Instead, the glowing coals and Christmas tree and you,
loaned telescope and moon so bright it made
the frosted garden ghostly day; a blue
moon which will gleam as other New Years fade,
till last, beyond my gate of ribs will be
this burnished full moon, at the core of me.

A blue moon is the "extra" full moon in years
that have thirteen full moons.

Wish

in the wheel of the stars
and the mow of the hay
in the blaze of amaze
at the birth of the day

in the whir on the wire
and the scorch of the sun
in the warm and the storm
and the world on the run

in the roil and the broil
of the clouds' heaving heap
in the indigo dusk
and the drifting to sleep

in the flap of a wing
or the bat of an eye
the slowness of Sunday
years scampering by

in the damp of the drizzle
the warmth of a glove
let there ever be you
let there ever be love

**THE LONDON
MAGAZINE**